PISCATAQUA POEMS

A Seacoast Anthology

Piscataqua Poems: A Seacoast Anthology
Copyright 2013 by RiverRun Bookstore

All poems in this volume belong to the contributing poet, and should be respected as such. Apart from small excerpts for review purposes, please do not copy, or reprint these poems without permission of the author. For more information contact info@riverrunbookstore.com

Published by RiverRun Select, and imprint of
The Piscatqua Press and RiverRun Bookstore
142 Fleet St. | Portsmouth, NH | 03801

Two dollars from the sale of each book will be donated to support the Portsmouth Poet Laureate Program. www.pplp.org

**RiverRun Bookstore publishes books!
Just like this one!**

We provide an easy, local, dependable way to publish your book.
For more than ten years we have been selling books in this community, and we know it to be a community full of creative people. We want to help you publish the book you've always dreamed of.

For more information go to www.piscataquapress.com or email info@riverrunbookstore.com

ISBN: 978-1-939739-00-1

www.riverrunbookstore.com
www.piscataquapress.com

Printed in the United States
Live Free or Die

Introduction

About a decade ago the admirable Maren Tirabassi, then Poet Laureate of Portsmouth, put together *Portsmouth Unabridged*, a collection of local poets celebrating all the things we love about the Seacoast.

For the past few years I kept thinking it should be done again, and then all of a sudden I found myself starting a publishing business. Well, no excuses at that point, so here we are.

Since *Portsmouth Unabridged* was published, a lot of things have changed. People, and businesses, come and go. The city gets bigger, and busier. It seemed important to me to indulge the idea that what we used to think of as "Portsmouth" we now generally refer to as "The Seacoast". We have expanded.

The poems in this book are loosely about the region I'll call the Piscataqua watershed: Portsmouth, Kittery, Rye, Eliot, Durham, and on. Oh, and of course, we must include The Isles of Shoals, which seem to burn brightly in the minds of all our local poets.

The poems were collected throughout the fall, and then read by myself and various co-owners of RiverRun and members of the staff. It was by no means rigorous or scientific, and we not only apologize to those whose poems weren't included, we apologize that not everyone won First Prize.

Speaking of First Prize, and of the Isles of Shoals, that honor goes to Kay Morgan and her lovely poem "Star Island Moments". We also gave a Second Prize and five, yes five, Third Prizes, because we wanted to and we are in charge.

The prize winning poems are at the front, the rest are in no particular order. We hope that you enjoy this selection, and we are so glad to have been able to make something that celebrates our local poets and supports the Portsmouth Poet Laureate Program. Enjoy.

~Tom Holbrook, RiverRun Bookstore

Contents

Star Island Moments	Kay Morgan	2
The Tide remembered	Maren C. Tirabassi	4
I, too, sing the Piscataqua	Mary Anker	5
Behind the Shed	Jane Vacante	6
Stroking Through Seaweed	Susan Kress Hamilton	7
River Birds	Marie Harris	8
Pulling Anchor	Charlotte Cox	10
Shores of Appledore	Ann Diller	12
River Haiku	Richard Brady	13
After News of War	G. Hanlon	13
Lost and Found at Strawbery Banke	Rodger Martin	14
When the Whistle Blew	Jane Elkin	16
The Friday After Tuesday, Sept. 11	John-Michael Albert	18
The Commute	Jane Coder	20
in the west end	Jane Coder	21
Star Island Rose	Beth Fox	22
Tide's In	Dudley Laufman	23
Covering / Uncovering	J. Dennis Robinson	24
The Geese at Plaice Cove	Cathy Arnault	26
Seagulls on Star Island	Cathy Arnault	27
Pleasant Street Encounter	Hugh Hennedy	28
Retired View	Hugh Hennedy	29
Rivers Parting	Patricia Corliss	30
there is a magic moment out at Seapoint Beach	Mary Anker	31
Swim on Star	Hugh Hennedy	32
The Heritage Chugs	Hugh Hennedy	32
At Fort Foster in October	Hugh Hennedy	33
From a Market Square Bench	Hugh Hennedy	33
we all board the new Gundalow	Mary Anker	34
late fall, 6:45 a.m., heading over the 95 bridge	Mary Anker	35
Beside the Piscataqua	Denise Hart	36
To a Worm Seen Before Radiation Treatment at Exeter Hospital	Kyle Potvin	37

The Promise	Pam Katz	38
the day after daylight savings ends	Mary Anker	39
Eeling with Carlie	Donald Young	40
Within Fort Foster in Mid May	Hugh Hennedy	42
At a Table of The Metro	Hugh Hennedy	42
From a Rocking Chair on the Oceanic Porch	Hugh Hennedy	43
For Charlie	Hugh Hennedy	43
(RE) BUILD THE RANGER	Donald Young	44
Day Before You Left	Rosemary Staples	45
The River	Susan Kress Hamilton	46
The Boy in the Marigold Shirt	Susan Kress Hamilton	48
Marcy Men	Tom Richter	49
Pine hill cemetery	Lori Pritchard	50
Baying at noon	Lori Pritchard	51
Peirce Island	John Simon	52
Skiing on Commet's Creek	Kay Morgan	53
In the South End	Hugh Hennedy	54
Still There	Hugh Hennedy	55
Walking in from New Castle	Hugh Hennedy	55
December Wedding in Prescott Park	John-Michael Albert	56
Suspiration	John Simon	58
Vaughan Woods	Ainsley Clapp	59
Glory Days	D. M. Ward	60
Five Frog Pond	D.M. Ward	61
Mourning Dove	Jane Vacante	62
Twilight at Adams Point	Kay Morgan	64
Downtown After the Physical	Hugh Hennedy	65
City of the Open Door	John Ferguson	66
Weird Tides	Kate Leigh	68
Rye	Kate Leigh	69
Lobsters	Kate Leigh	69
House Painting	Frank Cook	70
Elephants	Sue Reynolds	73
Meteor Shower—Strafford, NH.	Mike Dunbar	74
DECORATION DAY	Andrew Periale	76
The Tide Fable	Dudley Laufman	77

Odiorne Point	John Perrault	78
Star Island	Terry Karnan	80
The Place I Seek	Magi Leland	81
Abandoned Road	Dudley Laufman	82
Sonnet to A Walking Stick	Dudley Laufman	83
Sea Smoke	Marlane Bottino	84
The Parade	Marlane Bottino	85
Morning Fog on Memorial Bridge	Margaret A. Elliott	86
Paper Cranes over Portsmouth	Margaret A. Elliott	87
Memories Under the Bridge	Tammi Truax	88
Beneath This Bridge	Dan Comly	90
Summer Leaving Maine	Cleone Graham	91
The Sounds of Silence	Tammi Truax	92
Another Music Hall Memory	Tammi Truax	93
Strawbery Banke Forever	Tammi Truax	94
Returning	Grace Mattern	95
Local Politics	Maren C. Tirabassi	96
Missing Child Protocol	Maren C. Tirabassi	97
Oasis reflection	Maren C. Tirabassi	98
Ocean Views	Charlotte Cox	99
Appledore Island Poet to Poet	Barbara Bald	100
Walking with Gulls	Barbara Bald	101
Visit at Wallis Sands	Joann Snow Duncanson	102
The Surprises of Waves	Charlotte Cox	103
Portholes	Marie Harris	104
A Forest on Fire	Annika Barth	106
The Edge of the Dark	Marlane Bottino	108
Sea Smoke	Janet Sylvester	110
Currently	Karen Doyle	112
Memories Linger	Fred Pettigrew	114
Spirit of the Wentworth	Fred Pettigrew	115
Protest in Portsmouth	Pesi Jabre	116
A Mainer's Review of Her First Northern Californian Performance of Fall	Sue Reynolds	118
Coming Into Portsmouth	Patience Horton	120

PISCATAQUA POEMS

A Seacoast Anthology

Star Island Moments

I.

Fog wraps
around the island's shoulders,
shrouding her with silver mist,
gossamer, yet heavy.
Voices muffled,
faces wet with more than dew,
our boundaries blur, as we step
into the cloud.

                        II.

                        Lichen splashed on rocks
                        feels like velvet
                        under my thumb.
                        Spikes of goldenrod
                        thrust between gray ledges,
                        reach for the sun.
                        Strands of algae
                        undulate in tidepools
                        trapped in crevasses as old
                        as the stars.

III.

I sink into stillness
close my eyes, wait for sleep,
while whispers of salt air
and faint music of waves
sneak through the window
to kiss me good night.

~Kay Morgan
1st Prize Winner

The Tide remembered

>(originally several reasons to petition heaven
>to postpone the death of Robert Dunn
>now a memory of him)

I'd rather he only go out
so far that
he can still bring back poems.

But given that he's floated off Star
after reminding us
a door is open everywhere,

we must ask ourselves when it comes to a great
and beautiful conserving of good things—

who now will remember peaveys?
who will tap on typewriter keys …
teach us to talk to the listening forest …
who will tell the stories
of old fahts

or see garnets on the side of the road?

~Maren C. Tirabassi
2nd Prize Winner

I, too, sing the Piscataqua

I, too, sing the Piscataqua
swift carrier
of dreams
trade
tragedy

gundalows
tankers
lovers
ply your banks

in search of
an illusive good
like the ocean that feeds you
like the bridges that foil you

your danger and beauty
our current
our companion

~Mary Anker
3rd Place Winner

Behind the Shed

Pluck that raspberry. Yes.
At the branch tip.
   Subtle tingle as barbs
   birth such delicate perfume.

Palm, then roll it.
   Red globe revolving.
           Hand
   up to the sun
   that endows this world.

Don't eat it yet.
Flick off specks
from a passing phoebe.

Bend to the bottom
of the bush.
          Catch
silver hairs from fox;
wary sentinel all spring.

Now stand, open hand.
          Inhale
the heated red.
Then gulp it,
          miniature
   heart of late summer.

Best move on soon.
Yield.
     In deep shade
the bear snuffles–
impatient
     for his portion.

~Jane Vacante
3rd Place Winner

Stroking Through Seaweed

Swimming at high tide
surf crashing at the mouth of the harbor
Hurricane Bill skirts the
edge of Maine on his way to Nova Scotia.

Intense white, steely blue, loud, consistent
waves through the harbor, past the
trestle into the marsh.

I stroke through tangles of grasses and seaweed
pulled out by the force of this water,
cold but not frigid enough to curl your toes.

An eerie mist rising creates a see through curtain
at the edge of the shore—
the filmy softness of this veil defying
the energy and fierceness of the storm.

~Susan Kress Hamilton
3rd Prize Winner

River Birds

FISH CROW

Corvus ossifragus
croaking bone-breaker

grind of purple clam shell and
chew of rusted rocker panel and
spit of mussel hinge and
caw caw whistle of rising drawbridge
rattle of pebbles behind retreating wave
caw whistle caw of descending bridge
and hoot hoot horn foghorn fog
folding dark wings over encroaching night
clatter of anchor chain
mutter of moon light on shiny black

TERN

Sterna hirundo
sea swallow

Out of the glittering frenzy
at the Piscataqua's mouth
to nests on Isles of Shoals
one by one they speed
trailing invisible air-wakes:
bright white couriers
each carrying
in an orange beak
one silver message.

PISCATAQUA HAIKU

On outgoing tide
Double crested cormorants
Fall's dark outriders

~Marie Harris
3rd Prize Winne

Pulling Anchor

Those storm clouds boiling up like steam behind us
were not here this morning, even an hour ago,
when we began this ocean fishing venture
in a second-hand boat with rehabbed hull,
so certain of our skill and destination.

Now a vicious chop surrounds our little craft,
and we bless the strong brass anchor holding us
as we abandon poles to start the engine,
to make a run for land against the wind.
What, no homeward hum? No spark at all?

The old motor coughs and dies. He tinkers,
dropping tools. I pay out anchor line
because the swells are rising, eight feet now,
and the small boat's bow needs play to ride
the raging peaks and troughs that buffet us.

My mind's eye sees the anchor, gleaming darkly,
dug fast into the reef below, rock-firm.
But the swells are ten feet high and climbing,
and we pray each peak will break before the bow,

not swamp us as the boat lurches steeply
down between the monstrous water walls.
I've let out all the anchor line there is,
and still the sea towers, winds scream on.

Pull up the line, he yells! I can't, it's wedged,
I shout back, and if I do, we'll blow to Cuba!
Just cut it, he says, or the next wave will be our last!
I saw forever on the thick rope, picturing
the brass weight tight against the rocks below,

our safety and our doom. The last hemp thread
frays and snaps, the small boat rights itself,
and we give our fates over to the mercies
of the winds and swells, as we break free
and turn our sights toward the clear horizon.

~Charlotte Cox
3rd Prize Winner

Shores of Appledore

Oh salt in the air
scent of the sea
wind off the water
briny taste of nor'easters.

Oh eastern shore of Appledore
in the middle of May find a high ledge
out of reach from chill salt spray
watch wave after wave assault unyielding rock
dark water roil into white foam
sunlit drops soar skyward
an instant of separate existence
before falling back to rejoin
the enduring dance of deep waters.

Oh western shore of Appledore
on a foggy early morn squint through thick mist
almost glimpse Celia Thaxter
gathering fresh phlox and hollyhocks.
Later when bright sun blinds the ordinary eye
enter the shade of an old wooden shed
watch birders feed a tiny kinglet
barely alive after flying in from the Caribbean.

For swimming in the tidal pool
June's too soon
wait for high tide in July
even better August and September
bow down dive quick rise fast
Oh swimmer become the sea let it carry you light and free.

~Ann Diller

River Haiku

Standing close as one,
watching futures pass ahead,
rushing water sounds.

~Richard Brady

                    After News of War

                Tonight the waves creep in,
                linger

                in leopard
                skirts, soft reeding

                not a roar, and I who
                arrived glum am calm.

                One pounding scar
                of gold light on the wet

                sand disappears
                and I like disappearing.

                ~G. Hanlon

**Lost and Found at Strawbery Banke,
Portsmouth, New Hampshire**

(for Jack McCarthy)

Perhaps it was the waltzes--PJ's or Christine's---
lilting the curves of my ears, coursing like memory
of scallops, pasta, wine with a Tuscan scene.

Perhaps, the great sail of the bridge like an arbor
arcing into sunlight or some great silver fish
caught leaping from the solace of the harbor.

Perhaps it was the pale blue of the sky,
puffs of clouds whispering come, whatever the past,
come, for a moment we will soften the lie.

Maybe the *Albacore*—fat, squat, dry dock secure,
more Buddha than Shiva, smiling, "I'm not like others,
no weapons, find words on courthouse panels, reading's lure."

Or the desert-fatigued air crew from Texas, dinner at Newicks,
eyes like saucers noting lobsters carried as if a medieval feast: red,
steaming, formidable scorpions to those raised in dusty republics.

Maybe it was the dark beneath the trees, the equestrian bronze
of Fitz John Porter, general, cashiered long ago because he
could not kill men fast enough like proper American Khans.

Perhaps it was the old burial ground, face to face with the stone
of a wife dead in 1682. What can one say but, "Ma'm, I am here today—
a flicker of knowing, a link in the chain, but my life too is a loan."

Could it have been Strawbery Banke's summer-colored clapboards?
Four centuries making, squared into lawns, lovers clasping on benches
recessed among hedges while time naps in the orchards.

Or, lingering along the Piscataqua, ballast to the Navy's brooding
cross the water, Prescott Park, theater of flowers, a book full: tulip,
gardenia, iris, ranked, an Oz for any Dorothy's alluding?

Maybe all because a friend in the busy library read
from her trilogy, a half-century baked into words.
And the evening-after-party, me lost on circular streets
evolved when *grid* still meant grate, almost giving up
except a woman beneath a street lamps' soft radiance
carefully arranged her trash and said, "Ah, you must be looking
for Katie." And pointed, "Her house is down
that alley." What else can one do when the air
creates such Left Bank moments as these but zone
like a Turkish cat, a Van, warmth purring in its stare.

~Rodger Martin

When the Whistle Blew

Portsmouth Navy Yard
frigid island blight
cloaked in brick and grey
castle crowned, surreal
South End panorama

Roost of screeching gulls
nest of scurvy rats
petri dish of roaches
livelihood to over
half the folks I knew

Swarms repaired the subs
clattering down hatches
echoey and dim
all the day and night
save when I was there

Waiting for the whistle
everything was still
seven lazy minutes
watching for my Dad
the tall man to appear

Special treat on days he
didn't walk to work in
insulated pants I
called his puddle pants,
miles across a bridge
whose girders are no more

Early Yard birds fled
first in twos and threes
hustling past guards
collars up, heads down
streams of weary men

Khakis, work boots, caps
thermoses and sacks
weathered crinkly eyes
softening to be free
jostling through the gate to

Laborers' rewards:
sweethearts, supper, beer,
toddlers' sloppy kisses,
Cronkite, slippers, bed.

Who could ask for more?

-Jane Elkin

The Friday After Tuesday, September 11

We stood outside the Holiday Inn
on the Portsmouth Traffic Circle.
Seven o'clock in the evening.
Everyone held a candle in the parking lot.
The white aprons came out of the kitchen
and joined us. And a herd of bikers,
stampeding for Maine, pulled off the road
and joined us. The candles sputtered
their little lights against the dimming sun.
The text of the homily was known to all;
we needed no priest.

What do you do in this situation? You go on.
You welcome the famous poet. You usher
her out of the stale conference room,
outside where the world is banking
its September fires, and you stand with her,
and the leather-clad bikers, and the hotel
staff—high and low alike, housekeeper
and manager—and you go on.
It is the great theme of our planet: strangers, together.

Then someone said in a low voice,
barely loud enough to compete
with the flaming candles, the flaming sky,
"The bar tender would like you all
to have a drink on the house."
And we all sighed one more time
as if there could be an end to sighing.
The restaurant's votive candles
were extinguished. Everyone shook hands.
The motorcycles revved to a deafening roar
and slipped into the north bound traffic on Route 1—
it will be a moonless night;
they needed to make it to camp as soon as possible.

And that is the rite: Ite missa est. Pax vobiscum.
The mass has ended. Peace be with you.

~John-Michael Albert

The Commute

I liked best to drive in the early morning hours,
not westward toward dark mountains and black ice,
but east to Portsmouth
sea smell filtering through the vents,
coral and lavender streaking
a still dark sky
before sunrise
over Great Bay—
the Bellamy River,
brown and beige marsh grasses bent under early frosts—
some mornings mist rising
blurring all
in a gray haze—
a few masts
visible
from the bridges in Newington.

~Jane Coder

in the west end

Islington Street took us
to the west end
toward the plains

from downtown Portsmouth
beyond parking lots
covered in dust,

Robbins Auto Parts,
the American Legion,
cracked sidewalks,

Lease signs,
railroad tracks, Pic 'n Pay,
the Button Factory.

And after Route 1
in the side yard
of a New Englander built in 1911,

we saw a rose arbor
with roses climbing
its lattice

and a plane tree
with intense bark and wild foliage
in the front yard.

Two seats, like parentheses,
inside the arbor's arch
held us

in the west end.

~Jane Coder

Star Island Rose

A teacher with thorns
guides me to breathe in the salt
of shimmering seas
clamoring waves
that shape and sweep this island.

Green buds like little torches
wait to bloom,
welcome blossoms
that attract ants, bees
and other lovers to color and scent.

Petals drop, hips form
reveal in symmetry
the shapely lilt of stars
that have been there all along.

~Beth Fox

Tide's In

It's a game we play, see who says it first when we drive by
a salt water inlet like Johnson Creek there in Durham. Jacqueline usually
sees it first, but sometimes it's tricky, like in winter, ice piled up, or if the
tide is at half, is it in or out. Sometimes I am dozing by the time we get to
Durham but even in sleep I can feel the bumps on the road and know
where we are. Having listened to the tide report that morning at home and
subtracted the hour or so difference between open sea and Durham,
pretending to be asleep, I yell out "Tide's in." just as we round the corner
approaching Johnson Creek and Jacqueline says "You cheated. No fair."

If I am alone going to Portsmouth I still play the game.
Call up Jacqueline on the cell phone, say "Tide's in."

I wonder if she will play when I am not in the car or even if she will go that way.

~Dudley Laufman

Covering / Uncovering

I. Covering

Abnaki mother cries—
her child has died in birth.
Her Abnaki warrior breaks the Earth.
The child is wrapped in skins.
Small arrows are placed in the soil beside him for
                protection on his journey.
Red ochre marks this sad tiny section of the coastline.
The father with no children sees the tide is high
and takes his bride from the grave to shelter.
She is weak from giving birth and will not live the winter.
He carries his nets to the sea.
The little one is safe beneath, he says,
and sings a burial song while setting the nets.
A thousand years pass.
The nets are cast the same.
The coast appears unchanged, although the
                shore has crept up
closer to the grave where the Abnaki child lay.
In Egypt, a world away, the first pyramids are being raised

II. Uncovering

One digger shouts.
From all about the pitted field a dozen others
             gather around one hole,
perfectly square, each layer of sediment denoting time.
Within the flecks of iron ore, red ochre, Earth's blood,
the digger has found two tiny arrowheads.
No one will find human bone or reed baskets;
no cornhusk doll or leather casket could
             survive five thousand winters.
Only two projectile points embedded in sand.
Since the land has dropped further toward the
             sea, the workers scurry
suddenly and build a dam to keep rising
             water from the digging site.
That same day by the baby's grave, the sun now
             low and the tide withdrawn,
a digger comes upon new specks of prehistoric life.
With a tiny knife, and then a soft bristle brush,
he sculpts the earth from around a line of carved shells—
Venus clams, alternating violet and white,
once strung on bark twine, once hung upon
             an Indian woman.
Just a crude stone pestle is found
before the diggers pack tools and abandon the site.
Abnaki warrior, with no child or bride,
has pulled his nets from the sea and gone.

~J. Dennis Robinson

The Geese at Plaice Cove

The geese arrive,
Straining against a canvas of metallic cold sky,
A soft V,
Undulating like an unmanned kite string,
While roiling green waves,
Leave inroads on the sand below,
Mirroring the homebound pattern in the sky,
And reflecting nature's yearning,
To find an innate path,
That will lead to home.

~Cathy Arnault

Seagulls on Star Island

Surrounded by tide pools
And the spray of crashing Atlantic waves,
The seagulls swoop and dip
Over my sun warmed rock,
Their brown feathered babies
Alert and watching from a ledge,
Sensing the echo of a lesson
In their parent's cries,
The babies respond
Holding their wings aloft,
They fly in an arc over me
An insignificant barnacle on the rock,
And then back to the safety of the ledge
A stretching of the neck,
Beaks opened wide
Their parents screech,
In celebration of their offspring's dance.

~Cathy Arnault

Pleasant Street Encounter

Robert not thin but
Shockingly thin Robert
Why didn't I let you in

We talked of the Friendly Toast
Of poetry in town
In public places and more

I speaking clearly you not
O shockingly thin Robert
I said it was good to see you

~Hugh Hennedy

Retired View

It's a good thing I
don't live in this town
I'd never get any work done

the gray-sweatered gray-haired man
with glasses said in
passing in front of me through
the sun in Harbour Place
the river flowing inland behind him

Ants working behind me on
the wall's gray cap
one unable apparently to
rid himself of his frontal burden
even at the edge
the sky faultlessly blue again after rain.

~Hugh Hennedy

Rivers Parting

Separated,
separate,
and apart,
like continents in earliest times
These two
do not have oceans in between
but turbulence there is
and a persistent
pulling away from shores
that mark their boundaries.

So bridges must be built,
be they high or low,
be they wide or narrow,
to span their differences
and make their passage easy,
safe and sure to the other side.

~Patricia Corliss

there is a magic moment out at Seapoint Beach

there is a magic moment out at Seapoint Beach
the sun is missing at lowest tide
wet sand merges with dark floating clouds
both soaking in the dim light of dawn

my grandson and I tiptoe onto a cloud
slip off the bounds of earth
feel giddy and loose, free
dizzy from jumping one to another

looking down to look up
we're like the silver wings of sand pipers
skipping and skimming over the water
until we run right into each other

I swing him up to the sky
my offering my prayer
please let him find me always
up in those skies down in the sand

~Mary Anker

Swim on Star

So right away cold
you tingle

Thrilled you keep on
going until

The hot cold is at
almost your armpits

And now one two three one
two and

All of you is
in the lovely fire

And when you are out
the lone gull on the massive rock

Bays loud and long
agape

~Hugh Hennedy

                                                                   The Heritage Chugs

                                               Toward the departed bridge
                                               A heritage gone

                                               ~Hugh Hennedy

At Fort Foster in October

Lots of myrtle warblers by the shore
on the water a few gulls
a chickadee feeding on sumac
over the marsh crows excited
a pair of cardinals on a path
a calling jay

A man inquiring about woodcock

A black glove
pointing on a branch the way to go

~Hugh Hennedy

From a Market Square Bench

Could that be you Robert
Walking jaywalking hunched
Across sunless Pleasant Street

But you without a cap
And without that coat we knew
Cannot we know be you

If close enough for wondering
As we sit here observing
And thinking of you again

~Hugh Hennedy

we all board the new Gundalow

we all board the new Gundalow
the proud Piscataqua.
and with due respect to its ancestors
and daytime mission
we head out on its first June
evening entertainment cruise.
Portsmouth weather shows off
sun warm one last time
sky blues and lilac
revelry jams the decks
puts us in a feisty mood
we leave them grounded
laughing and waving
we tack into the wind
anticipating the bridges
Kent Allyn and Joyce Anderson
sing and fiddle us east and west
we dance with the crew
do-si-doing
swinging our partners
singing to the past
to our loves here and gone
to our city, our river, our home

~Mary Anker

late fall, 6:45 a.m., heading over the 95 bridge

late fall, 6:45 a.m., heading over the 95 bridge
the sun purples the sky
until it burns through the horizon
and the bridge disappears over the Piscataqua
my car floats the rest of the way across

at school I kneel down
next to the boy at his desk
trying to shrink my authority
we hover over his halting words
until he looks down and away

heavy backpack, 5:20 p.m., leaving the hollow behind
I swerve off campus
the eastern sky is violent with color
as stunning as the continuing failure
that burns both him and me

~Mary Anker

Beside the Piscataqua

This river, silvered ribbon that
        carves earth,
pushes forward
until the tides reverse.

Push back, churn the waters
              turbulent,
life-changing
           life-giving.

The river's gift is its daily story
       of flow and change
    push ahead, receive back
How does the human heart open to receive?
       To fall into change, confident
            of floating?

~Denise Hart

**To a Worm Seen Before Radiation
Treatment at Exeter Hospital**

little inchworm twisting on your thread
Spun high above the blades of grass below.
You twirl, you stretch, you arch your compact form
As nimbly as a circus acrobat.
You pivot in mid-air for gasping crowds,
Which dream, but do not dare to fly like this.
Yes, you, dear Worm, are braver than the rest,
You flip and bend without a trace of fear,
So grateful for this chance to dangle free
And pause your measured pace across the earth.

~Kyle Potvin

First published in *The Lyric* and in Kyle Potvin's chapbook *Sound Travels on Water* (Finishing Line Press, 2012)

The Promise

That spring shall follow winter

Regardless of the nights still edged in ice;

And bring a joy particular

To all things in the process of becoming.

~Pam Katz

the day after daylight savings ends

the day after daylight savings ends
we hurry across darkening
Seapoint and Crescent beaches
around the piles of freezing seaweed
slipping on piles of slanting stones
our shoulders stiffen into the wind
the November cold surprises us
but not the full luminous clouds
greys widening the sky
as dark moves in
depleting and enveloping us
minute by minute

~Mary Anker

Eeling with Carlie

Carlie was blind; well, he was legally;
But, if he held his wrist up to about two inches
Away from his eyes, he could tell you what time of day it was.
But he had other ways of telling time
And getting on in the world which saw him as handicapped.
If the sun were out, he could orient himself to it and know the hour.
When in earshot of the barn he could tell by the lowing of the Ayrshires
If they were anxious for the afternoon milking.
He was a herdsman for Big Doug.
He lived on River Road and had his house and garden plot,
As well as all the milk his family needed, as part of his work arrangement.
In the winter he liked to hike the mile—down past Annie
                Scammon's, where the road turned to dirt—
To the Town Landing and do some smelting or eeling on the Squamscott.
Neil and Wayne would carry the axe and eel spear; their father
                brought the gunny sack.
Little Doug and I tagged along to see the whole enterprise.
You could go at high or ebb tide.
Both times of the lunar pulsing of the river through the bays to the ocean
Were good for eeling— but low tide was better.
"Safer to get on and off the ice", Carlie said.
Plus the lower water level put you nearer the prey.
We went below the Ox Bow where there was a sandy bottom.
Chopped a hole in the ice—the chips sparkling in the sun like a diadem.
Carlie probed the bottom, pushing the multi-pronged spear up and down
                as he felt for his supper concealed in the eelgrass.
Now jabbing furiously he hoisted out the spear with one, or two,
                or even three squirming, wriggly eels,

Thrashing their streamlined bodies, sleek and glistening;
These intrepid, daring swimmers, New World Argonauts,
Who managed odysseys far beyond our imaginations,
                yet returned here to this their home.
We'd get a mess of 'em. Wouldn't take long.
 "I like 'em rolled in corn meal -- fried in a skillet", Carlie grinned,
His faded denim farmer's cap perched at a rakish angle;
Anticipation spreading across his face.
We trudged back in late afternoon in time for milking;
The sun lowering in the West behind us.
And since that day of eeling near six decades ago,
Enlightened by the discovery that there are trees
Whom I consider friends,
I further realize now—
Those eels were my brothers.

~Donald Young

Within Fort Foster in Mid May

While the bright blue steel of their backs
Tree swallows probe the air
The glossy ibis works the marsh
A farmer bent on planting

~Hugh Hennedy

                    At a Table of The Metro

                    How these chairs shine
                    handsome in the light of
                    candle and lamp

                    Polished wood slanting bank
                    in lines as clean and curved
                    as bombazine black

                    O slim conjoined staves
                    upholding the slim bridge
                    of the back

                    Songs of pastoral care
                    in this dark resting place
                    this day

                    Illustrious serpents
                    bringing the garden back
                    by way of art

                    ~Hugh Hennedy

From a Rocking Chair on the Oceanic Porch

Jesus Christ you can see the bridge he said
Having sat there for a good fifteen minutes
Before lifting his eyes over the old
Cemetery and the blue-gray water to note the arch

~Hugh Hennedy

For Charlie

On this breezy afternoon by the river
the wires of the drawbridge
sing like cardinals
or would so sing
if they and the wind
could learn the rhythm
comorants and cardinals know

As it is
one comes to understand
they make the electric chatter
starlings make

The river meanwhile
roaring like elephants
the flags snapping like fire

~Hugh Hennedy

(RE) BUILD THE RANGER

BUILD THE RANGER—build her fast—
Unlike the bigger ships put speed
Infused in keel, and ribs, and mast.
Labor hard with skillful hands to shape her creed.
Designed with Yankee craft and cunning care,

THE RANGER—let her size belie,
Her speed and daring—courage rare.
Enlist a crew that's young and spry.

RANGER—honored with an ensign new,
And captained by a man who's brave;
Now furnished with a steadfast crew,
Go forth and dance upon the wave.
Engage the foe across the main—
Rigged to fight, and fight again.

~Donald Young

Day Before You Left

One last look.
To think people cursed you when you were up and
when you were down.
I for one will miss you.
A friend raffled by the wind.
Salty phantom moths
flew from the Prison, ate away at your beauty.
For some it was just rust-Ick!
The moon still shines
over the empty place.
I wait for a new you,
 a new view,
a new memory,
a new Memorial Bridge.

~Rosemary Staples

The River

A bicycle on pontoons,
the rider pedaling hard
across the current,
against the tide
of the great river—
a big smile, we circle and he is gone.

Hot summer evening
on the Piscataqua
a white wooden launch
putts through the chop,
and two schooners near the lighthouse
under sail are silhouetted—another time.

There are so many fishermen
in one small green skiff,
so heavily laden
as to dip the rail,
a couple in an old lobster boat,
search for the rumored eagle's nest.

The gundalow passes by
crowds aboard waving
at the four women in
green and purple,
headed toward a quiet spot
to watch the sunset, and share supper.

We raise our glasses
to old friends, to women,
to the men who cycle across country,
who motor alone up the coast.
Absorb the sea freshness
the warm air, the setting sun…

As we come in,
men are fishing in a line
on Frisbee's wharf,
illuminated under the bright new dock lights—
"Warning: don't get squid ink on the dock,
ruins it for the rest of us fishermen if we aren't careful."

Squid by the bucketful,
carried by the warm Gulf current
all the way to the Maine coast,
as we watch,
young Asian families mingle with old salty locals
catching the bounty of a summer evening.

~Susan Kress Hamilton

The Boy in the Marigold Shirt

The boy in the marigold shirt
tapped to the beat of the boombox
but mainly to his heart,
on a wooden platform dragged where
the crowds are,
in Market Square,
a slight knowing smile as the young girl
dropped a coin in the jar —
"Ain't no sunshine when she's gone."

The sun hit my cheeks as he grabbed my heart,
tears uncontrolled onto the brick walk amongst
all those strangers, the marigold energy was winning.

~Susan Kress Hamilton

Marcy Men

The great river sways first back then forth
at the head of the harbor 2KR flashes in three second flourishes
inward the flow reverses like crazy irish women
born of the tide...of the interminable human tide
of the long long crazy ride
held hostage by some old piece of leftover pride

The Marcy Men are lowering the street
over the great sewer force mains of Old Rivermouth
the machines of destiny have arrived and are at your door
the boss has given you the rope of success or failure
more machines may arrive based on the ebb and flow of construction
seventy year old sidewalks are being systematically replaced
with new conveyances of unsung passage

Still the Marcy Men toil over the line and grade
they become history just as easily as long long ago
the hardscape tends to remain where the flesh will fail
still the Marcy Men prevail
the streetscape is given over to the souls who build
and the unfortunate kid that was killed

The Marcy Men toiled on
small machines did big work
hand shovels and brooms seemed to be all that were needed
love and fairness were understood but still argued about
and the line and grade continued down the Marcy Street
it ended finally with the end of a career
it ended with an end to an end
it ended with the end of the Marcy Men

~Tom Richter

Pine hill cemetery

I search for the oldest trees   the darkest stones, slate
The weather could not diminish
Enter the canopy - waiting   A mother died
This sister   dear   a widow separate
With siblings   lost.   A sweet angel carved for infants grief
A Ham and Peasley   a captain's Wife.

I lay paper on each name   each carved angel and skull,
pressing graphite to stone   and rub into relief
Lydia   Mary   Elizabeth
Hundreds of days of years emerge
Seventeen hundred and thirty five.
Seventeen hundred and eighty one.
Seventeen hundred and seventy five.
I rub the hand chiseled stone   into the year 2012
Into the year of my brother's death.
I rub the face of angels   skulls and ornament
A wreath of flowers   a heart   all stone.
And names   another name I do not know
But understand the longing for

In the distance   the sound of trains and bells   traffic
And the rush of living.   Still
beneath this fine conifer   tended to watch
the dust of bones taken up   into cones above   that drop
A seed of what it is i am
We are   yet living.

~Lori R. Pritchard

Baying at noon

If I sit on the shore
Stuff my mouth with salt grass
Bury my feet   toes
Bare into the mud.
Certain delving into earth

And sink   sink amongst the mollusk and small fish
Minuscule fish all gills and breathing

I pretend   I can be from here
Of here   as if   perhaps
May be   I come from this cove.

~Lori Pritchard

Peirce Island

No wonder so many fall—indeed,
the wonder is what keeps upright
the tallest of these trees given the scant
overlay of soil on this granite extrusion
tied to the community by a short, arched
bridge over a backwater of its tidal river.

The warming of its blood under the summer
sun interrupted by our approach, sensed
through the compacted earth of the footpath
or rock beneath it, the snake animates,
becomes the familiar S, and is quickly lost
to these eyes and the dog's nose.

Restraining interest at the end of a leash assures,
in this instance, the continued well being of canine
and serpent, affording the latter an opportunity to shed,
and in leaves fallen beneath those trees with
               the tenuous grip,
leave another skin, and the now prostrate dog
once more to dampen the carpet under his muzzle.

~John Simon

Skiing on Crommet's Creek

Sometime last night, otters
slid down the frozen bank,
splashed into the winter creek
where they hid under the ice,
away from curious eyes.

We glide across the ice bridge
over their heads, slipping,
sliding, our skis askew.
The top layer cracks, shatters,
shards slip off the floe like panes of glass.

To the otters, it must sound like the breaking
of a thousand goblets, or the end of their world.

~Kay Morgan

In the South End

Crossing the fifth bridge
One saw seven egrets
Standing in the mud of
The South Mill Pond
Where it started hereabouts

Though one is tempted to do
Things with the birds and the mud
The fair needs foul sort of
Thing and tempted to push
The fives and sevens hard

The fact is the egrets
Were and are the thing
That needs no doing north
Or south then or now
Their whiteness being enough

~Hugh Hennedy

Still There

Going up the stairs and knocking on
Terri the Tailor's door
I could have been Raskolnikov
Jacket concealing the hatchet

Good thing I wasn't he for she
The good tailor would have sized him up
And cut him down in no time at all
Instead of the almost two weeks

She said she'd need before she'd have
My broken zipper fixed
The zipper in the pants I bought
From the hunting folks in Freeport

~Hugh Hennedy

Walking in from New Castle

If one were running
One probably would not
Hear the gulls
Much less the terns
Announcing to
The comorants
The end of the world
Over and over and over

~Hugh Hennedy

December Wedding in Prescott Park

I went to a wedding on Saturday last:
a party of five, including the Rev.
The double-barreled Alberta Clipper from Friday,
bitter cold wind and the first snow, both calmed.

And we stood by the wooden warehouse
in the tracks of Portsmouth's old dry-dock:
something about dragging ships from the sea,
scraping off barnacles,
recaulking their seams with hemp and tar,
spiffing them up for another twenty, thirty years—at least.

Poetry was read, a modern service was read—
no "dearly beloved we are gathered" or "and obey."
The bride laughed when the groom recited his vows,
a lifetime of frustration and doubt released
like steam into the waning afternoon light.
The rings were made by a mutual friend,
who had no idea he was performing such a sacred service:
there, in his studio, he free-handed wind-swept trees
into silver with an invisible saw,
his four-year old deep in mischief at his feet.

We retreated to the couple's house for pistachios,
cheese and crackers, champagne and hot tea—
don't forget the hot tea—
before the party trundled to *The Green Monkey*
for a sublimely crafted meal, nearly overlooked
for the open and passionate conversation,
heightened by a generous host
and by the golden light within.

I went to a wedding on Saturday last,
which was as it should be:
start at the bare part, the cold part,
shot through with savage winter light.
Start in a desperate huddle with friends,
by a familiar green bench,
the bride holding a bouquet of holly and cedar.
And let things grow from there.

~John-Michael Albert

Suspiration

The orientation is wrong, what should be vertical
horizontal, horizontal vertical,
felled by some frenzied fury of air,
trunk and limbs prostrated, exposed,
gnarled roots groping in vain for nourishment
above a half-cup shaped depression at the base
full and empty at turns, as rain falls
and seeps into soil from which roots still buried
absorb what the branches need to leaf out,
the leaves to unfold, transform, and fall
the short distance like that between lovers' hearts.
What came then shrieking to dice the living trunk?

Many months after the act the segmented corpse
remains, fed no longer, feeding what it can,
the air aquiver with belated lament, a dirge,
reprised for as long as life and love lost are mourned,
spun of wings shimmering gold in the afternoon sun.

~John Simon

Vaughan Woods

I can hear them
the memories
the yelling with joyful delight
as little shoes run down the dirt covered hill
I can hear the continuous whines
fading with age
I can see the tread marks
from slipping feet down to the water's edge
with worried-eyed parents behind
I can smell the water and know it's not
far I remember the family
the togetherness
I remember my unwillingness to go

I see you now from my quiet perch
wind sweeping through my short cropped hair
your tree dancing to the soundless music
overhanging the glass water
the sun sliding down the sky
hiding itself
you are timeless
watching the comings and goings
history flashing before your eyes
you watch silently
everlasting
never going
never leaving
never gone
imprinted in my mind

~Ainsley Clapp

Glory Days

This time of year
This late summer time
This time between a high dry heat
And beginning of a crisp, early fall
When the days begin to shorten
And the cooler damp nights lengthen
When the ground is moist and verdant underfoot
Late flowers still blooming
The cone flowers, back-eyed Susan's, golden rod
Resplendent in this glamorous light
Of an Indian summer still swarming with bees
Butterflies and dragonflies swoop across the pond
Water hyacinths a glory of tangles in green and lilac
Frogs jump from lily pads into water deepened with koi
Rampaging vines succulent with heavy damask grapes
The old pear tree limbs arthritic and bent to the ground
Under the weight of fruit
And tonight under the glow of a waxing gibbous moon
I will sit in silence listening to the
Late summer thrummings of crickets
And watch for shooting stars

~D.M. Ward © 2010

Five Frog Pond

I built it
With my own hands
Dug the ground and leveled it
Sweat stung my eyes
Sticky thighs and sunburned neck
Hands grew calluses, nails were broken
Spirit not
I built it
Laid the stones,
created steps
For the waterfall
Where now three years on
Quan Yin sits serenely
As water cascades down
To the lilies and the hyacinths
I built it
A bench for my father
Now four years gone
Where we sit side-by-side
In the quiet eventide
As I tell him of my day
And how I rebuilt my life
Surrounded by skimming dragonflies
Bees and butterflies
And green-headed frogs
In my five frog pond

~D.M.Ward © 2011

Mourning Dove

Spring

So late; Spring melt, rising green.
Hollow remnant by the steps
like an ovoid of white coral.
Light breeze passes through it.

Summer

I love to coax her from the air
scatter seeds on brick paving
link her even more to earth;
my dream of constant music.

Fall

Close the windows to a crack.
Let tawny smoke and ripe-
leafed air seep in
and quavering song recede.

Winter

Air shuffles and shakes snow
but cannot budge
the small grey mound
snugged in by the bluestone steps.

Spring

Windows just opened–
dove passing in flight.
Hear the wind whistling
through her.

~Jane Vacante

Twilight at Adams Point

Single file we traverse the swampy trail,
step from jutting rock to exposed root,
focus on feet in the gathering dusk.
You stop: see a deer kneeling in the marsh,
antlers branching, back like a velvet boulder.

You develop the drama: an arrow whispered through reeds, pierced the
buck's side. I remain silent,
tacit assent to a story I don't believe.
Here you also saw ivory-billed woodpecker,
a Louisiana bird believed extinct.

Reluctant to go closer, we walk on,
avoid poison ivy, reach dry ground.
Looking back, I see a thumbnail moon
and the marsh mirage. Crows shriek their version
overhead. We could argue, but we don't.

~Kay Morgan

Downtown After the Physical

Are they newly painted or
Have I up to now simply
Been walking past not
Noticing these settings
Of the doors at the front of the church?

Beyond the massive columns
Those paneled and arched settings
Hooding the recessed doors
Like the wimples of nuns this church
Has never recognized.

Even if frames and doors
Are really newly painted
I find myself at this
Stone Church aware of death
Restoring again my sight.

~Hugh Hennedy

City of the Open Door

I come to visit America, travel by bus.
My mother say be careful, is dangerous place
but that's not true, even for me.
I don't speak English
but Americans go out of their way
to be kind to visiting man from Africa.

I have my cell phone—
it understands Swahili.
That's a joke. Americans love jokes.
I tell my mother I will call her.
My mother wants a code
so she'll know I'm all right.

Remember the story you read to me
when we were all much younger
about the billy goats and the bridge?
The little one goes across, "Bim, bim, bim,"
and the second goes, "Bam, bam, bam."

When I call, if I am a little happy,
I will say, "Bim, bim, bim."
And "Bam, bam, bam"
if everything's very good.
And if it's better than that,
watch out old troll!
The big billy goat gruff
is taking America by storm!
"Bom! Bom! Bom!"

I'm riding on an American bus.
I teach you my English word:
Swahili basi, American bus.
You say, "Basi is bus!"
We are in Maine
We are heading for "The City of the Open Door."
Everyone is so friendly, so nice.
It wouldn't surprise me if they
are waiting for me when I arrive.

Get ready, get set, say,
"Bom, bom, bus!"
And we laugh and laugh and laugh.

PORTSMOUTH, N.H. — Police said the 10-hour drama that paralyzed the center of this seaside community and pitted a phalanx of federal and local law enforcement authorities in a tense standoff with a man suspected of carrying a bomb was merely a misunderstanding.

A passenger on the bus thought she overheard a black man making a cell phone call about a bomb. She used her phone to call police. The man at the center of the ordeal was an immigrant from Burundi who spoke no English. There were no explosives on board, and the middle-age foreign national, who refused to leave the bus for seven hours after his fellow passengers had safely exited amid heavily armed police, was apparently nothing more than a frightened bystander with little idea of what was happening around him.

May 8, 2010

~John Ferguson

Weird Tides

Lazy waves with crushed velvet underbellies,
Crinkled silk froth at the mid-tide shoreline.

Dented by approaching storm clouds, the
        Pink horizon warns, with
                Distant slashes of rain,
Fully undaunted.

Across your grey-green back,
        My vision streams to the Isles of Shoals,
                From the clipped New Hampshire coast
At Wallis Sands..

This is a day for water spouts,
Spontaneous cyclones and weird tides.

~Kate Leigh

Rye

A charm bracelet of lights
On the eastern rim
Adding more charms
As the day grows dim

~Kate Leigh

Lobsters

Long strand of bedraggled ponytail down your back,
Orange tee shirt pulled over alpha chest and spine,
Blue jeans hang like the roofline of an old barn,
Feet wrapped in worn-thin black high-tops.

You fetch a two-handled metal pot of seawater,
Lug it up the mossed path to the house to
Quickly boil fiddley bare lobsters in brine.
Their hibiscus shells crack in our hungry fingers,
We feast on fresh shell-fish flesh.

Later when the moon looms amidst the heavens
We return the remains to the sea, swash out the pot,
Plop ourselves down on the porch rockers, rest and digest,
Overhung with a vast quilted blanket of close starlight.

~Kate Leigh

House Painting

I set out here to write a poem
        about the painting of my home.
A task I took upon myself
        (why should I pay someone else?)
For a simple task that I could do,
        to change my house to gray from blue.
It's probably best that all should know
        my father-in-law's a painting pro.
Tall bridges, buildings, steeples, more,
        a man of skill, of Portsmouth lore.
So that on the day that I announced
        my plan to save our bank account,
My wife just said with doubting look,
        "Let's just have Dad come take a look.
"I know he will and do just fine.
        Do twice the job in half the time."
"He surely won't," I said, insulted.
        "Won't paint my house! Won't be consulted!"
"Just gray on blue, it's easy to do.
        I'll be the chief, you'll be the crew."
Another doubting look appeared,
        followed by sarcastic sneer.
I shrugged them off with smile bright,
        knowing she was wrong and I was right.

Now the house in need was two floors high,
        with peaks that reach into the sky.
My plan was simple, as anyone knows,
        to first paint high then down below.
So one fine day with pail and scraper,
        I climbed up and began my labor,
And found out as I neared the sun,
        the laws of painting: Number 1.
Your ladder should be tall enough to
        reach the very highest stuff.
A ladder that's too short and shaky

        tests less your skill and more your bravery.
To stand up high on tippy-toe
        and stretch out far as arm can go,
Is to invite all sorts of strife
        and, of course, a shorter life.
Nevertheless I flailed away,
        changing blue to darker gray,
Madly swiping beyond my reach,
        splattering paint into the breech.
When suddenly there's noise that's foul,
        a cry from crew and angry scowl.
"I see some drips and places bare.
        You're dropping paint into my hair.
"Your work's a mess, it's not like Dad's,
        his work is good and yours is bad."
Now patience is a virtue, true,
        but has its limits with a crew.
"Don't worry," I said, "T'is drips of gray,
        you're turning that shade anyway."
And here I ran afoul Rule 2:
        and something you should never do,
There's really nothing worse or badder
        than angering she who holds the ladder.

That tiny little tiff aside,
        I went around the other side.
Again I climbed upon the ladder
        and found an insect even madder.
Now it's time to state Rule 3:
        "Not all insects live in trees."
Wasps sometimes build their nests
        where you can't see the little pests.
And on this point I am intense,
        a waving brush is no defense
Against a wasp on revenge bent
        because of a little accident.
I wasn't trying to be a louse
        by sticking my ladder into its house.
To give a chance to calm it down,
        I chose to help my wife near ground.

Despite her look of stormy weather, I said,
    "It's great, we'll work together.
I'll paint here and you down farther,
    we'll finish quick." (Without your father).

We'd best discuss rule Number 4,
    "Pay attention to this chore."
A bit of paint not far enough flung
    could end up on a ladder rung.
And a slippery rung is much a hazard
    to those whose egos might get shattered.
It's true I missed a little splatter,
    so when I climbed that pesky ladder,
I slid on spot of slippery paint
    and plunged from rung with ankle spraint.
Then there came an awful sound,
    paint hitting me, me hitting ground.
As I lay there on the grass,
    and felt my ankle swelling fast,
I could have sworn I heard near me
    a small and smothered "Tee, hee, hee."
My wife came o'er to check my health,
    and found me mostly mad as hellth.
She smiled down and said just right,
    "Guess you were wrong and I was right.
And judging from the spill you've had,
    I believe I'll just go call my Dad."

~Frank Cook

Elephants

    For My Grandfather at The Cabin "Up Country"

After supper, my globe-shaped grandfather fed paper plates
to his ample-bellied, black wood stove that gathered the paper in
with its million blue lips, roaring, satisfied, trumpeting flames.
Crowned again, the stove sleepily huffed smoke up its chimney,
while grandfather lumbered into his worn corner chair
and trumpeted to sleep beneath a cloud of hay-tossed, silver hair.

~Sue Reynolds

Meteor Shower—Strafford, NH.

I looked the Universe square in the eye,
The black pupil cataract with stars.
That night, in unpolluted Strafford
I could swear the broad, unblinking lens
seemed somehow sad and shier for the staring.

A couple years younger than me, she reclined,
And, in the field, reduced to nearly none
But fundamentals: the color of her hair,
A Celtic crown, and a body dark as
Space between the lights above our town.
We heard the coyotes crying in the distance,
But she didn't bat an eyelash at
The sound. I think the only time I'd ever
seen her sink her eyes was when they ran
The obituary in the paper:
Dead, after long battle with
Cancer of the lungs.

Somewhere is a flower pressed inside
A yellowed book, *Quantum Mechanics*. It marks
The spot on Heisenberg a student read,
and forgot, still, lost upon a shelf.
Smothered, buried,
pristine, preserved.

No one's ever closed a star-shot in
A book, thank Christ. But I, once, knew a pair
who caught and closed one in themselves,
Neatly pressed between the swimming sheets.

If light is such as we, here, understand,
Then for a splintered instant stars were dead
to all who looked too late, but lived a little
longer, softly tinted blue and brown,
In our still, New Hampshire town.

You can't know both location and momentum.
The more precise the one, the less the other.
Action in relief is no activity at all;
unless, of course, the medium has some motion of its own.
So, if, some night, you feel particularly
Brave, go out and do what we have done.
Dare to look the way you did the first time you looked up,
           until the weeping starts, the movement
Moves, and again begins the fall.

~Mike Dunbar

DECORATION DAY

She leans back against
the tulip tree
cool, shadowgazing
at sunbathers bobbing
on a sea of grass.
Beyond, the bridge to Kittery
rises, welcoming sailboats.

The book in her lap—
The World's Great Religions—
promising connection, unity,
seems less compelling here
where a child asks to be picked up
and a butterfly tattoo,
seeing sun for the first time,
seeks magnetic north.

~Andrew Periale

The Tide Fable

A man and woman poled their narrow bateauria on the outgoing tide to an island in the marsh. At a narrow passage they grounded in the flat. She got out to push but sunk to her ankles in the mud. With great effort she managed to pull herself free and get aboard. He got out to try his strength and sunk to his knees. But he too got back on board and they sat there waiting for the tide to change. They saw six herons pursued by a hawk. Gradually the tide started to rise releasing the boat and they polled their way to the island. She kneeled in front each stroke hiking her jersey, revealing the white dory of her waist. Somewhere I love you lurks in the reeds very close to the surface. The tide had come up enough for them to go swimming, washing off the mud. They spread a blanket under a tree and had some strong Islandian wine and meat and bean rolls. The poleing and wine made them sleepy. When they awoke the tide had turned again. She hurried to retrieve the boat before it floated away. He had an eye for the roll wind coming their way. It would be a tough pole against the tide and wind. Apia was furthest from their minds but it will rise again.

~Dudley Laufman

Odiorne Point

Odiorne—shaggy—the way I like it:
Leaves skittering down the trail,
Sticking on stalks, catching on thorns;
Humongous oaks creaking, soughing—sumac
Shivering—taut ropes of bittersweet
Throttling the ragged cedars;
And this pine-needled wind unraveling
Thread-bare clouds, exposing my seventy—
Year-old eyes to the blur of the blinding ocean out there.

So much for glasses—off they come and look:
A quivering wild tangle
Of bush, perfect for some painter
To tease out a stag or two—some poet
To imagine the naked huntress
Aiming her bow. And who wants
To know how it ends? Rose tinted lenses
Went out with the Sixties—but on this Point,
This time of year, things appear more fragile, frames or no frames.

Just south of here, mansions clutter the coast:
Sculptured lawns surround gated
Temples guarded by granite walls.
No one home these days. Only landscapers
To keep the master's keep well-ordered—
Keep the elements in line.
As if nature ever follows orders.
As if the breakers aren't building offshore.
As if the ground will never shift beneath those foundations.

English sailors dragged their boats up this beach
Back in sixteen twenty-three—
The year the Pennacooks began
Slowly disappearing into the woods.
A hundred years on, and all but gone.
David Thomson held the deed.
The Pennacooks never held anything
Save wampum and pelts and game for winter.
Never taxed themselves beyond a need—winter costs enough.

Winter wants your bones. Another few days,
Odiorne will be buried.
But not today. Today's a gift.
No need to hurry. Still time to visit
The one grove I like to think is mine.
That visits me when I sleep
With a flutter of leaves over my eyes,
With a soughing of limbs above my head—
With vines winding around my dream, tying me to the earth.

Season of shagginess then. Call it that.
And I do: for the dead leaves
Piling in ditches—the milkweed
Casting loss to the wind. For the old man
I just came across scuffing along
The trail under creaking trees,
Under woolly skies, nodding to the sedge,
Weaving himself into the sheer fabric
Of fall. Watching. Waiting. How clear it all is to me now.

~John Perrault

Star Island

At night fall
Lanterns light the path
Up hill to the chapel.
Inside wild flowers
Adorn window sills and altar.

Outdoors the quiet sea sounds
Echo against ancient tombstones.
A stark obelisk stands in memory
Of Captain John Smith.

Across the way Celia's garden
Resurrected, blooms.
Overhead the squawk
And squeal of gulls
Nesting in the rocks,
Fiercely fighting
Off predators.

The wide welcoming porch
Rims the old hotel.
Its rocking chairs keep time
With the waves.
Guests wander down
Paths between cottages.

In the distance White Island's
Beacon flashes.
The waves recede and surge
Sun-dappled.
Always the wind sings
Through the grass,
Sweeps clear the rocks,
Scatters foam beachward.

~Terry Karnan

The Place I Seek

Quiet is the place I seek
Beneath the heavens' celestial roof.
Where croak of frog
And warbler sound.
Where moss grows think upon rock
And marshes welcome fawn.

Serene is the place I seek
Beneath the heavens' celestial roof.
Where lilt of loon
And thrushes dart.
Where moon beams charm
Mornings crisp and clear.

Tranquil is the place I seek
Beneath the heavens' celestial roof.
Where roar of surf echoes deep;
Bass and blue fish feed.
Where beaches ebb in the wild
and hearts soar at dawn.

~Magi Leland

Abandoned Road

I never think of myself as abandoned. Gates and Bars maybe but not abandoned. Even though there is an end to me (I come out someplace, someone's back yard), I am long and have history in my mulch.

I have stone walls on both sides. I dip down deep into the dark forest. Road to long ago, trod on by natives, deer-skinned musket carriers. Penacooks jogged to hunt, colonists to pioneer. I just go to go.

I am on the map. A dotted line weaving through the elevation curves that makes me famous. About halfway I am pinned on a pasture high as a crow's caw.

At one point I merge with an exempt railroad track. The engineers used my foundation where I followed the straight and narrow through a gorge with blue ice. I don't think of trains. I am a tunneling green wreath.

The trains veered off onto a switchback so it could gain the hill. I go straight up the steep incline into the edge of town.

On the return I see what the eyes in the back of my head missed before. Cardinal flowered herons by a brook. Old logging road (no stone walls like I have). Cellar hole with lilacs near the high pasture (They must have wanted the view). When the farm failed I was closed. There was a better way to get to town. No jeeps or wagons now. Snowmobiles, ATVs, and horses, hunters and foot traffic. Here comes one now knapsack and walking stick.

Sometimes I wish I went to a tidal inlet but that is another road.

~Dudley Laufman

Sonnet to A Walking Stick

Someone found my walking stick – they held
it in their hand, probably at work,
even though I thought I hid it well.
I could not find it after futile search.

Of course it will have changed into a snake
if touched by someone other than you or me
or next of kin. *Might have been mistaken*
for the brush pile or tossed out to sea.

Before that happened though, change occurred.
The stick became a reptile in the night.
Somewhere on the island, sea vetch stirs,
and it slithers on the edge of tide.

If I watch it carefully, grab it quick,
it will change back to a walking stick.

~Dudley Laufman

Sea Smoke

I've seen you float silently
like an owl through the pines,
unfold your pale wings
and leave mystery behind.

I've seen you billow
like mountains from the sea,
and I've seen those mountains
walk smoothly to me.

I've felt your breath,
cold and damp from the deep,
make warm summer days
disappear like a dream.

Yet when you surround me
with clouds of soft white,
you reveal another world,
like a prism to light.

~Marlane Bottino

The Parade

The sky is bluing in patches as rain clouds lift
on Halloween day—the air is warm, very warm,
and the sea is shining diamonds by the shore path.

Couples walk hand in hand, their silver hair blowing,
as white caps rise in the balmy wind and dogs run by,
big dogs, little dogs, dogs in sweaters—smiling.

Strangers greet me with friendly hellos and shared
perceptions, given face-to-face and eye-to-eye,
with spoken words and easy, natural connections.

Halloween night, the moon is full over the river,
green paint peels on the bridge, thick steel rusted red—
water shining under our feet, walking to the parade.

Halloween revelers travel shoulder-to-shoulder,
families with babies, bright costumes flapping,
children with neon necklaces and big round eyes.

Ink blue clouds fly past the moon, the wind rises,
bronze leaves shake in the street light, witches march,
witches on stilts, brooms pounding, little dogs in costume--smiling.

Monster couples stride side by side as robots chirp,
a boom-box rocks and troupes of zombies dance to "Thriller,"
zombies moon-walking for a swelling crowd—cheering.

Old graying monsters, black, white and young monsters—
let us face our fearful monsters, and embrace them.
Let our spirits come together, parade and dance.

~Marlane Bottino

Morning Fog on Memorial Bridge

Sea smoke masks
the bridge beneath me
as I sail across the river
on a misty cloud.

Bottomless brick buildings
rise before me,
floating above
a froth of fog.

What lurks beneath
this downy blanket
covering my world?

Anything is possible—
      Celtic selkies?
      Sea monsters?
      Poseidon himself?

Soon the sun burns through
the gauzy curtain
separating my world
from the unknown below.

The drone of a distant tugboat's horn
awakens me from my half-dream.
A quick peek beneath the bridge
confirms that all is as it should be on the river.
Any mystical creatures have evaporated
like the morning dew.

Margaret A. Elliott

Paper Cranes over Portsmouth

Paper cranes float over Portsmouth.
White origami shapes
flutter in a clean blue sky,
aviators sent up in hope
and in remembrance
of a century-old document
signed with dreams and promises
of a better future--
sentiments as fleeting
as the thin breeze
that holds
the delicate
folded papers
aloft.

Margaret A. Elliott

Memories Under the Bridge

With the bridge as backdrop
my husband and I would sit
on a blanket in the park
sharing picnics and plays.

Now he is dead and gone.
When he was but a boyfriend
we sat drinking beer on a deck
at a restaurant, also erased.

Laughing, we watched kids jump
from the bridge, the Coast Guard
almost immediately arriving to scold.
Later, I'd bring my children here;

my daughter's sixth birthday party,
a flitter of fairies in the garden…
her childhood now rippling away,
as unstoppable as the tides.

A few moonlit moments with others,
the nothingness of our togetherness
rode off on patiently waiting waves.
Later my old poet friend Hugh and I

would sit on his balcony, watch
the bridge go up and down
while we talked of art and literature
and what he had seen washed away.

Gone, also, is he now.
My life.
Tugged away.
Memories under the bridge.

Until at last
the bridge itself gave way.
As if to say
it could bear witness no more

to watching what was
swirl out to sea.

~Tammi Truax

Beneath This Bridge

Here, beneath this bridge,
where thundering steel
lifts travelers over the river,
a stone bears his name.

Shaded by towering
concrete piers leafed
with green girders,
this stone tells that he died
here, beneath this bridge,
working on a summer day,
at an age (only twenty)
that makes me wonder:
what did he leave behind?

~Dan Comly

Summer Leaving Maine

Cars jamming turnpike
Piscataqua arcing bridge
Summer leaving Maine

Raucous Waxwings flock
Celebrating late berries
Flee cold northern winds

Leaf peepers invade
Blind window buses speed by
The trees ignore them

Afternoon setting sun
Cove reflecting orange leaves
Turning-tide pauses

Quickly plucked blossoms
Capturing colorful riot
Before early snows

Quiet empty beach
Lobster boats head out pre-dawn
Mainers hunker down

Cord wood neatly stacked
Storm windows are all in place
The patient stove waits

~Cleone Graham

The Sounds of Silence
(Great Bay Feb. 25, 2008)

The invisibly slow unfurling of
thawing birch bark, snowflakes
decrystallizing in the bright sunshine,
a sudden micro-movement
from above of an old limb
dying just a little,
the slow tired ripple of
what had once been a wave
finally reaching the shore,
the odd underwater plinking of
ice sheets shifting in the shade, and
the quiet orchestrated cacophony
of ten thousand dead brown leaves
dancing on their branches in unison
at the baton of the breeze off the bay,
as the plea of the woods real residents
politely whispers with the wind,
"Please go, leave us, in peace,"
and ushers me out.

~Tammi Truax

Another Music Hall Memory

I saw something tonight
under Frank Jones' undoubtedly
grateful gold ears,
while the comforting harmonies
of my childhood rose up
to baby blanket me in the balcony
under the beautiful new – old ceiling.

I saw David Crosby tap his heart …
three rapid thumps
of his plucking fingers,
sending a special counsel
to the relatively young bassist
just stepping up to bat.

"Play it from here",
he seemed to be not saying,
giving the kid a code
that he can live by,
teaching the child well
that his father's hell

did slowly go by,
and feeding him
on his dreams.
I looked at them and sighed.
He touched my heart.

~Tammi Truax

Strawbery Banke Forever

So named they say
because the *banke* offered up
abundant plump berries
upon the arrival of

the scurvious Europeans
who came, and built
and fished, and fought
and loved, and lived

the place into *Puddle Dock*,
while ship after ship brought
scores of soldiers to the shore
trampling the last precious *bery*,

and adding to the heavy refuse—
natural, architectural, human—
used, then abandoned, tossed aside,
until the sisters Prescott, with a stomp

of their righteous toes, said, "Enough.
Let us clean up this unholy mess,
plant flowers to remember, and
restore order and honor to the *banke*."

And build they did, a pretty park,
where people stroll, and sit,
but can only imagine how sweet
those *berries* were in 1630.

~Tammi Truax

Previously published; Albert, John-Michael, Ed. *The 2008 Poets' Guide to New Hampshire*. *NH*: The Poetry Society of New Hampshire, 2007.

Returning

My friend sits on a dock
of happiness, her own address.

Here my planks are bleached
black, heaving into splinters, silt

dark slabs along the channel's
shoulders. Marsh grass pastures

independent green, thousands
of gull nests, screaming nesters.

The tide's pirouette is simple;
I wait for the shift of chart lists,

high line creeping later each day
until a morning with a gap,

this basin is full just before midnight,
just after noon. Emptiness

is one approach to memory,
the long sweep and churn.

~Grace Mattern

Local Politics

"I've been putting up signs
for my brother-in-law --
he's running for Register of Probate,"
says the woman in the library basement.

We have been discussing
a murder mystery called, *Primary Season*,
and how it tries to capture
the frozen quadrennial craziness
that is New Hampshire.

We have all decided that DuBois
has nailed it—
with the phone calls and the traffic,
the secret service
and the endless coffeetunities
to meet just about anyone.

It's all about the hopeful and the hectic,
cynical old journalists on their cell phones
passionate college students
living in rehabbed school buses.

Another says, "I work the polls,
and folks around here get just as worked up
about ballot items and road agents
as whose butt's going to
warm the chair in the Oval Office."

A quiet one says, "local politics is just like this,
... well, without the murder."

"Maybe," we all laugh.

Another says, responding to someone,
"I've seen all the signs."

~Maren C. Tirabassi

Missing Child Protocol

I walk through the woods, maple, birch and oak,
calling out, not expecting to find him—
the boy who's gone missing, possibly
in need of medical assistance,
sixteen, they say,
suicidal, they say,
then in a rush—height and weight, eyes and hair,
blue sweatshirt, ball cap, Christopher.

October woods under clouds heavy with rain
are filled with clandestine sound—
small animals,
the settling of logs,
the winds rustling up the crumbles of the leaves—
all around a small conversation
of all hallows eve, all saints, all souls,
that we do not understand.

I wade through wetland and the thickness
of all that has died,
of next spring's mulch,
but no young man wandering,
named for the saint who carried Jesus
on his shoulder across a stream.

I call out once more, then turn,
pray for souls, travelers.

~ Maren C. Tirabassi

Oasis reflection

I should not be here—
and if I am, I should never admit it.

After all—the mall in Advent?
The crowds, the sales,
bellringers, clerks in santa hats,
elders on scooters, teens checking their wallets
outside Aeropostale, the Gap—
how fashionable it is to criticize,
easy to mock.

But I am arrested
by the sweetness in all these faces
sitting to rest around me
in the Food Court,
in these days when gold is in short supply,
and the shoppers display more
tattoos than frankincense.

And here I sit,
eating a pretzel across from Old Navy
and a cell phone store,

watching a caravan of people
alight with that old desire
to make a journey,
find a gift, and offer it,
however myrrhly inappropriate.

And yes, they have coupons and
gift receipts and grumpy kids,

The straw on our knees is easy to spot,
not so much the star.

~ Maren C. Tirabassi

Ocean Views

Side by side we sit, looking
out at the far rim of the ocean,
close to the edge where each wave
hisses up near our toes, and
peace rolls in to wash over us.

Together, we seem near sisters,
shoulders touching. I say, I love
having nothing but water and sky
in my eyes – it makes my head
lean back and my breath go deeper.

She says, It always disturbs me,
not being able to see across.
I say, What? She answers, Lakes
are so restful, you know, where you
can see the trees across the water.

I ask, What about that feeling
of freedom you get from seeing
no limits? She answers, That's
what I get from being able
to see to the other side.

~Charlotte Cox

Appledore Island
Poet to Poet

The island bookstore displays her work—
Celia Thaxter's poems, letters and stories—1894.
Amid reconstructed gardens of dahlias, hollyhock, cosmos,
we walk hand in hand—me in zip-off pants,
                she in petti-coated skirt.
Celia offers a taste of island life.
Herring gulls guard chicks, scold interlopers.
Waves spray granite ledges, tides meter the ebb and flow.
Foghorns, sounding for eons, punctuate cool night air.
Struggling to craft a poem, scribbling free verse in a new age,
I hear sisterly suggestions for rhythm and rhyme.
Our footsteps fade into a future that came and went.

~Barbara Bald

Walking with Gulls

Boardwalks, splotched with uric acid,
                white as dribbled paint,
stretch before me as I scramble
over granite rock toward my island dorm.
Gulls—Herring and Black-backed, share my path,
at times blocking my progress.
In summer sunlight we stop,
puzzle at each other, eye to eye.

A mother positions herself between me and her chicks,
chicks as large as she, wearing mottled coats
                of fledgling feathers.
They squeal for regurgitated meals, prodding mother's beak,
insistent, relentless.
Overhead, perched on roof tops amid island scrub,
fathers scold, warn, chatter in chorus with other sentinels.

I speak softly, reassuring no harm, seeking connection.
Always, I stare—memorizing hue and form –
white plumage, yellow beaks with red food spots,
stubby legs, plump bodies, flesh-tan feet.
They waddle before me, beside me, another
                species, eyed close-up,
traveling this planetary road.

We share a mutual look, cautious stance, not sure
what to make of one another.
Like a pup, offering its vulnerable neck to another,
I glance away, averting eyes so as to not threaten.

Wishing I could decipher their calls, calm their caution,
understand their ways, I will, upon departure,
miss these gulls, miss their companionship,
                however tenuous,
like I would miss my own shadow.

~Barbara Bald

Visit at Wallis Sands

I had a visit with Millie today—
thought she might like some company.
She doesn't know me, and all I know of her
is what is written on the plaque affixed to her bench:
    Millie McIntyre, 1920—1995,
just enough to tell me that she loved this place;
probably spread her blanket and set up her favorite
beach chair here on this sand more times than she could count.

She saw sand castles rise and fall with the tides,
countless holes dug by small hands wielding tiny shovels,
suntanned lovers sharing towels barely large enough for one—
a scene playing over and over again like a welcome,
never-ending encore for a favorite seaside symphony.

Today Millie, Betsy Bacon, Paul and Claire Davis,
and the others, keep watch here from their
memorial benches lining the pathway between
the sod and sand—offering weary beach goers
a place to rest while collecting one more
seaside memory before starting for home.

Once our visit ended, I drove away from the beach
with some of the names on those benches still shining
in the rear view mirror of my mind—Albert Grande,
Thomas Bonano, Arthur and Esther Gray, Mary Matossian,
Richard Lyons, Vi and Clif Gilman, Marjorie Moreau Forbes,
the Gaults . . .

The days are growing shorter now and winter will be coming on,
yet we have no need to worry about our Wallis Sands;
Millie and her faithful friends will surely watch over
our seaside treasure, keeping it safe until we meet again.
After all—they loved this special place, too.

~Joann Snow Duncanson

The Surprises of Waves

Ocean surges, sunshine dances,
light plays on the pockets of smooth sand
between the age-old boulders scattered on the beach.

That brief time of surging forth
could be the length of a human lifetime, striving,
reaching, transforming, slipping back, reorganizing.

Only the rocks stand firm,
as the eons sculpt their minute changes,
while the sand flexes and regroups with every wave,

And one Speedo-clad old man
with strong legs, browned skin, furry back,
climbs (by god) barefoot over the impassive stones –

May he not let his sinewy foot
be caught between the hulking hoary boulders
and bruise or break those tender matchstick ankles –

yet he springs deft from stone to stone,
then reaches a smooth space and pauses, breathing,
before he leaps, grinning, to the next knot of ancient rocks.

~Charlotte Cox

Portholes

*

Hail hammers the deck.
Green leaf-rags fly by.
Framed: a bleacher of gulls
on shore, hunched,
waiting it out like loyal fans.

*

Bow nudging into a northwest wind.
In the port porthole: sunset's outrageous oranges.
Framed In the starboard port,
a sky-ground of pinks,
soft blues and grays,
and the Barley Moon...
celestial STOP at the end
of a corduroy road of yellow light.

*

Dawn washes the glass with pale light.
Nothing stirring. No need to stir.

*

September afternoon. Glimpse
of winter. Departing terns.
Silver chips on a dark cumulus field.

*

Moored in the river
tonight, alongside a river
of highway, upriver
of bridges and buildings,
there is only light.
Without sound.
Without consequence.

*

Below, I glance up
from rinsing a tea mug and spoon
as an incoming tanker slides its length
in rusty segments across the glass oval,
close enough for me to see a sailor turn
and start back toward the deckhouse
four stories high. A common sight.

Then the Coast Guard boat. Flashing blue light. Siren.
Uniformed young men with guns.

Please stand off! Please maintain
(what is he shouting? how many yards?)
distance from the incoming vessel!
Are you the owner of the boat?

Yes. This is our own small craft
riding a fair wind on a slack tide
in the Piscataqua,
approaching White Island Light
on the afternoon of September 12th.

Sorry to bother you.
Have a nice day, Skipper.

~Marie Harris

A Forest on Fire

A spark is carried on the breeze
Where it settles amongst the leaves.
Unseen. Unnoticed. Unaffecting.
But slowly, quietly,
The brisk winds come
To breathe life into that tiny spark.
It blooms across just one leaf,
Before it skips to the tips of another.
Up through their stems it spreads;
The reds,
The oranges of flame.
No longer a tiny spark,
It is dark,
Deep, bold and remarkable as it flourishes.
Now the fire is upon us.
A conspicuous sight
Are the radiant, rampant flames
Trailed by a fiery path
As they expand across the land.
Their hungry fingers engulf the trees
They lick the bark
And set ablaze the leaves.
From all around the people come
To witness a forest on fire,
To see for themselves
The flaming, blazing, brilliant colors
You don't find anywhere else,
To see the warm fiery glow
That smolders bright and rich
In the treetops below.

And while some burn on,
Others melt away
But the fire is here to stay.
Down to the floor the burning embers sway,
They coat the ground in a liquid fire,
A lava glaze
That matches the intensity,
The richness and purity
Of the treetops still ablaze.
And every year an autumn spark
Carried on the breeze
That settles amongst the leaves
Gives the forests a warm fiery glow
That only the people of New England know.

~Annika Barth

The Edge of the Dark

In winter, every light in the dark is sacred,
but as I stand on the edge of the woods, I wonder.

The snow-draped and bent-shouldered hemlocks holding watch
over my house look like ancient sleeping wizards.

If I walked away from my tight roof and my warm fire,
if I walked into these deep woods without a light,

I would feel bone-chilling cold, and startle at sounds
made by creatures more afraid of me than I of them.

But if I could quiet myself within, and could breathe
the wildness that is life, and become one with the air—

would a hemlock wizard shimmer in the darkness
above me and quietly let me know the truth

of who and why I am? Would that message be
even more terrifying than a silent universe?

In winter, every light in the dark is sacred,
but as I stand on the edge of the woods, I wonder.

The snow-draped and bent-shouldered hemlocks holding watch
over my house look like ancient sleeping wizards.

If I walked away from my tight roof and my warm fire,
if I walked into these deep woods without a light,

I would feel bone-chilling cold, and startle at sounds
made by creatures more afraid of me than I of them.

But if I could quiet myself within, and could breathe
the wildness that is life, and become one with the air—

would a hemlock wizard shimmer in the darkness
above me and quietly let me know the truth

of who and why I am? Would that message be
even more terrifying than a silent universe?

~Marlane Bottino

Sea Smoke

Frost on a window, indistinguishable from roses
knotted into a curtain, burning
      as blue dawn drains into it
      from the backyard apple, its parabola
 of ruddy spheres
what's left of summer. Across the fence, a red boat's dry docked,
buttoned against snow
      that won't arrive until later.
      Warming your hands
at a cup of coffee
in the kitchen, you send your wish into the hemlocks, and
beyond them, to the bridge
      that takes you away, commuting days.
      You want to root here,
into the water's going
and coming, to be home, to be home, in this old place
long skirts hurried
      through to the small barn
      a Mexican restaurant worker rents
now. Instead, you layer sweaters,
walk out to scrape ice from the car, coughing, like luck, into drive.
Past the Square that plows
      have already heaped into drifts,
      you slide onto the bridge
and—how can it be worded--the braiding tensions of the current,
the light the world flows inside,
have turned to precious metals.
      Every register of platinum
      and rose gold issues into
the frigid channel, coaxed

by sun into thermal plumes, bright steam cooling to droplets bent
by air into pyramids—
        dozens of them—
        seemingly still. You
stop, idling for minutes
to let the bridge raise, then drop; the day's first fruit, a form of fog
exhaled by water,
        already gone, as
        the future accumulates
in the rear-view mirror: an apple tree,
dirt-brown, disappearing into the chapel of its vanished leaves.

~Janet Sylvester

Currently

If born overlooking once strawberry-laden banks
in the dead-end of New Hampshire winter
just shy of emerging crocus
alongside still ice-encrusted
muddy bottomed mill pond
stagnant lilac bushes
barren birches
inhaling initial breath
infused with raw salt-saturated chill

it appears inevitable
that forevermore throughout
a run-of-the-mill native seacoast lifetime
there will course an incessant
and fathomless current
of connectedness
with this piece
of atlantic tidal treasure trove

the river itself
swift venous reminder of
all that moves continuously deep within
and propels us
outward to the open sea
      and it's vast uncertainty
dispersing it's confluence of ancestral echoes

those lifetimes that came before
historical tales of yore
sent downstream via brackish contributory fingers
into and expansive estuary
the run-off from great-great grandfields
pastures and forests of the Squamscott
gathered amid ripening cornfields and sunset illuminated
salt-marsh meadows

tugging us back toward
safety of familiar harbor
customary ebb and flow
wondering how much might arise
during the next slack tide

either way
the river does not have time
to perseverate
as it eventually maneuvers around treacherous rocky points
willfully gliding over a granite graveyard long submerged
and ingrained in all vessels
it sustains

~Karen Doyle

Memories Linger

A gathering of towns surrounding a small city
Born of river and sea
That smelled of burning leaves in the fall
And
Salt air—sharp, familiar, and comforting
Year round
My roots are here—at the corner of Lincoln and Elwyn
Youth—rain streaking down a window pane—willing me to leave
And away
A small smooth stone sent skipping across waves
ripples catch the sun, and cast reflections into my eyes
Falling asleep to the music of loons—clear cold water
A world of perception and packaging where sawdust covers all sins
A clock measures seconds—slowly, and years pass quickly
Some questions are never answered—never meant to be
Returning to the soil where I began
Finding the goblins had left, and never returned
And the hills are not as steep
This city hasn't changed much
But—what became of the boy
A tiny light—still part of the show
And memories linger
Seaweed and barnacle covered rocks
Cries of seagulls
Coarse sand
And the sea—always the sea

Fred Pettigrew

Spirit of the Wentworth

Unseen, they linger by day and by night
In stairwells, corridors, and ballrooms
Greeting each new guest with proper formality as they pass
New guests, who dwell upon the excitement of today
And may be unaware of past glories
Unaware of those who once visited and left
Leaving a part of their life ensconced within these walls
While forever longing to return again and reclaim their memories
Unseen are guests, young and old, gentleman and ladies—
Waiters, waitresses, bellboys, and cooks
Handymen and innkeepers, entertainers and owners
Dressed in formalwear, tennis whites, and uniforms of their trade
They have returned again to calm salt air, seagulls, and the cry of the tern
Returned to flowerbeds, winding paths, and quiet places to sit
Returned to fishing and swimming, tennis and golf
To carefree days and magical nights—oh, those magical nights
Returned to sailboats answering the breeze, lifting to ocean swells
Casing spray sparkling into the sun, a fleeting imprint upon the sea
To sunrises from the sea in the East, and day's end sunsets in the West
With clouds tinted red, gold, purple, and pink
Returned, yearning to rediscover a summer love lost forever
at seasons end
And—enduring lovers returning to this place where they began a lifetime
together amid sun, sea, the perfume of flowers, and
the sensuous rhythm of the evening dance floor
So as you walk these corridors, stairwells, and ballrooms
listen carefully
Above the murmur of voices, the clinking of ice on crystal,
the swish of garments
Listen—as these walls faintly echo an orchestra tuning
You may not see the past
But they are here with you
Dancing silently in the evening air

~Fred Pettigrew

Protest in Portsmouth

Coming of age in the '60s
Meant smoking pot
Hanging my bra
In Goodwin Park
From the cement fingertips
Of some forgotten war
Hero
Watching *The Real McCoys*, *Bonanza*
Or *Hogan's Heroes*
And the Flag draped caskets on the news
So many of them
My Rebellion came naturally
So that hip hugger bell bottoms
And a red bandana
Were my protest
I'm cool
Smoking Marlborough red box
Tasting acid under my tongue
war protesting is all the rage
And then came
My Alex
Paratrooper wounded in Nam
Morphine injector and serious pot-head
My first love, not my last
Slowly dying in a New Hampshire prison
He becomes my peace protest

My rage
The flag draped casket
Is my Alex
As war turns real
The Death and destruction
Aren't props any more
And the Friday nights in Market Square
I'll be holding my protest sign
But my face will be turned down
As if my shame would show
And my secret thoughts
Would be revealed
As I thank some God

That I have no sons…

~Pepsi Jabre

A Mainer's Review of Her First Northern Californian Performance of Fall

Act I. October

What kind of production *is* this,
To play it all so bald, dry-eyed,
bare limbs splayed akimbo
across a motel-beige mosaic
not a lick of spit on your lip,
your last whisper
a dusty, limp-wristed drift off
under a blank headstone,

while back East, the Old Queen
is going down fighting in glory!
She sweeps to center stage,
sets her hair on fire, and
hisses mists of champagne
across the black velvet firmament!
It's her build-up to the build-up
of the grand finale's colorful furor
before the curtain drops. Bravo!

Act II. November

I was wrong about you.
after that pallid death scene
and the soft applause of one simple, long rain,
you've sprung right back,
spreading a green grin across the valley,
feathering every crevice with evidence
of your rise from the dead.
Stunning!

While the Old Queen has required
tedious months of total silence
under wraps and cold packs,
a good, long steep in a recuperative sleep
before she deigns to stick one
tiny, hyacinth toenail out
to see if the world has yet warmed
to the idea of her green reign again.

~Sue Reynolds

Coming Into Portsmouth

With the hum of tires on the grid of the deck
Of the bridge, Max looms
        Dressed darkly with
        Buttons buttoned to his neck.
Across the river, at the Shipyard, the Coast Guard
Tracks an oncoming ship

New at sea, Diego, offshore, and done swabbing
Watches fish and dolphins fly through the wake erupting
From the cut and pass of the great ten-thousand ton *Jin Qiang*,
A freighter with bulk cargo destined for New Hampshire
Where cranes and loaders will lift her salty content
        Onto the pier
        Into piles
        And onto trucks for next year's snowy season
At night he feigns a sextant
With longitude, clock, and scope
To fix upon the Northern Star and pretend he is
More than unlicensed, and is home and not daydreaming.
Sextant north and east by thee with graduating arc,
He knows he will never prime and paint fast enough
To stop the salt and the rust spreading there

A deck cadet and motorman pass behind him at the rail.
A hot-tipped cigarette tssst is flicked into the sea.

All week long, Max has waited for a ship
To come into his harbor and glide under his bridge,
An old green, cantilevered bridge
        With center span rising
        And the warning horn sounding
        And a hundred cars waiting
He sees a ship as magnificent and huge
As the full moon drifting past the windows of a tall office building

~Patience Horton